Journey
to a
Miracle

Ruth L. Griffin

Unless otherwise indicated, all Scripture quotations are taken from the King James Version (KJV) of the HOLY BIBLE.

Contact: rltbychrist@yahoo.com

ISBN: 1481172441
ISBN-13: 9781481172448

DEDICATION

This book is dedicated to my daughter, Denell, whom I love dearly. I thank God each day for giving me such a precious jewel. You are a woman that loves God, has embraced the Lord and made Him master of your life. Witnessing the faith you operated in for Kayla's life during such a difficult time; inspired me to share our story.

This book is dedicated to Kayla, my sweet darling and courageous granddaughter who displayed bravery and strength through this trying time of her life. I love you deeply and thank God for sparing your blessed life. You are beautiful, obedient and destined for greatness.

God performed a miracle in Kayla's life, and for this, to Him I am truly grateful and inspired. To God be all the praise and glory! This amazing miracle of a journey that took place, we receive as nothing less than a wonder of my God who has never lost a battle, and never lost a case.

"Journey to a Miracle" is my testimony and witness that GOD still performs miracles.

Trust in the LORD with all thine heart; and lean not unto thine own understanding. In all thy ways acknowledge him, and he shall direct thy paths.
Proverbs 3:5-6

ACKNOWLEDGMENTS

First I give thanks to Father God, Jesus, and the Holy Spirit for the awesome miracle and answer to my prayers. God you are so miraculous. I love you!

To my sister, Della, thank you for writing the forward of this book. You are the best!!!

To my brother, John, his wife, Joyce and church family, thank you for your consistent prayers and support.

To all of my family & friends, thank for your encouragement and unconditional love.

To Apostle Brown & Pastor Gayle, I am truly blessed to be under your care receiving your love and wise counsel. You have been a great relief to my family and I over the years. I especially appreciate all of your help rendered to complete this God glorifying book.

To Keynia & Tricia thank you for your editing skills I am most grateful.

Table of Contents

FORWARD

But thanks be to God, which gives us the victory through our Lord Jesus Christ. I Corinthians 15:57

Certainly, we acknowledge God's abundant miracle of healing, in spite of the enemies' ferocious attacks on this Godly family. The enemy is not slack or timid in his use of his weapons to destroy those he deems frail in some area.

Never has God relinquished His omnipresence in the face of ungodly, devastating and discouraging situations of His people. When we wait for the answer to each test of our faith and hope, God emphasizes through His word that He will never leave us or forsake us. In Psalm 27:10, David wrote, "When my mother and father forsake me, then the LORD will take me up."

Paul also reminded the faithful people of God in II Corinthians, 4:8-9 that, "We are troubled on every side, yet not distressed; we are perplexed, but not in despair; persecuted, but not forsaken; cast down, but not destroyed." God's people, through prayer and perseverance causes us to say like Job 13:15, "Though He slay me, yet will I trust in Him. I will maintain mine own ways before Him."

Job 23:10 says, "but He knows the way that I take: When He has tried me, I shall come forth as gold."

This book is a reminder that God has not stopped performing miracles. The author presented God's very sensitive and personal work in the lives of both her daughter and granddaughter. She is fully aware that God not only worked miracles in the Bible, but over and over through this period of time, she witnessed him working a miracle for her as well. It provided an unshakable faith in Him.

CAN GOD? YES GOD CAN.

Dr. D.L. Clinton – Th. B.C.C.

JOURNEY TO A MIRACLE

"But Jesus said, Suffer little children, and forbid them not,
to come unto me: for of such is the kingdom of heaven." Matthew 19:14

CHAPTER I

The Emergency

June 5, 2002

The miracle began on the same day in history as another historic event that occurred 35 years prior to the day: the Six-Day War. This event where four of the most powerful Arabian enemy nations were defeated by one nation, Israel, was reckoned worldwide a confounding miracle, because of the odds of it happening. And with the odds being stacked against her, God gave an eight-year old girl a profound miracle on her birthday. This miracle created the same degree of astonishment to all who knew her. The following are chronicles of our journey to the Miracle as told by me, Puffs' grandmother.

Puffs, a beautiful bright little girl with big brown eyes and long black hair, lived with her mother, Denell, in Jamaica, New York. Though Puffs' birth name is Kayla, the nickname stuck with her as when she was a baby Denell combed her hair into two neat Afro puffs. She always looked so cute with them. As a child, Puffs attended a Christian elementary school and was always happy, reading, writing, and drawing pictures. Puffs had always been a music lover from the time she was a tiny tot sitting in her car seat. I recall that whenever she heard music playing she would rock back and forth. But if the music ever stopped, she would make a short, grunting sound to indicate that she wanted the music to be turned back on.

Her mother, nicknamed Denie, is a hard working young woman who commutes daily from Queens to New York City. She loves the Lord and would make sure to take Puffs to church every Sunday, especially because Puffs enjoyed the choir so much. To me it appeared that Puffs always easily learned the songs the choir sung. The Sunday experience, as told to me by Denie, began on the Sunday leading up to her 8th birthday. She said, "I vividly remember watching Puffs walk down the aisle when the preacher gave the alter call because that was the Sunday Puffs went up to the altar, gave her heart to the Lord, and received a certificate of her salvation." Denie later told me that the whole bus ride home that day she and Puffs kept singing over and over again the song they heard the choir singing: "No matter what the weapon is, I want you to know that I win." We didn't realize how prophetic in nature this song really was.

Puffs had begun complaining of headaches days prior to that Sunday experience; and we also noticed that she hadn't been able to keep any food on her stomach. This caused Denie to become quite concerned about Puffs' health; and as a result, she took her to the pediatrician who diagnosed her with a stomach virus. The medication he prescribed for the virus did not seem to be helping because the symptoms did not leave. Up until then, and even after the Sunday experience, Puffs still was not feeling very well. She did continue to attend school even though the vomiting increased and headaches continued. We knew something more was going on when one day the school nurse called for Denie to pick Puffs up because apparently her equilibrium was off. Puffs even admitted that while in class the words on the blackboard seemed to be jumping off the board. That day Denie immediately left the job rushing to the school to pick Puffs up. Denie said that even when she had taken her outside to catch the bus, Puffs was complaining that the sun was bothering her eyes, so much so that she had to buy her a pair of sunglasses, that didn't seem to help the situation.

Wednesday, June 5, 2002

That same week, Denie had become so upset about Puffs' condition that she called me at 3:30 in the morning; though we didn't answer. She later told me that when she called that morning the phone had just rang and rang. My husband later admitted that he did hear the phone ringing, but didn't pick it up. At 6:30 a.m. I actually heard the phone ringing and answered to the sound of great worry in Denie's voice on the other end. "Mom, Puffs threw up again at 3:00 this morning, and I want to take her to the emergency room. I want you to go with me. Puffs is losing weight. No matter what I try to feed her, soup, water, nothing is staying down."

Still half awake, I managed to get dressed pretty quickly. The morning rush hour was in full swing and was bumper to bumper from the suburbs of Long Island to Queens, New York. Once I got to the borough of Queens, I called my daughter once I arrived reaching her at 8:25 a.m.

When I got their the neighbor's dog started barking. I noticed Puffs coming down the stairs without her jacket so I shouted, "Puffs go back in the house and put your jacket on; you can't come out like that!" She immediately turned around, and did as I asked. When Denie and Puffs finally got in the car she asked, "What hospital should I take her to, Jamaica Hospital or Queens General?" I hesitated, and before I could answer, Denie had responded that Jamaica Hospital was closer. So off we rushed to Jamaica Hospital's emergency room.

After we registered Puffs at the front desk, the nursing staff checked her blood and vital signs. The doctor that examined her was a thickset African American woman named Dr. Shepherd who later came out to speak with us. She was surprised that Puffs' blood work had returned normal and that she was not dehydrated. However, she was concerned that Puffs was weak, had headaches, looked very sickly, and had an imbalanced equilibrium. She said, "We're going to give her a MRI of the head just to rule some things out." Thank God she did because by 11 a.m. we were shown what was happening inside Puffs' brain. Dr.

Shepherd called both Denie and me into her office to look at the X-ray pictures of Puffs' brain. We could see that something about the size of a peach was covering part of her brain. We could not believe what we were seeing. Dr. Shepherd explained to us that a tumor was lodged in the cerebellum of Puffs' brain, and that this tumor was the cause of her headaches. Hearing this information made it clear why she could not keep any food down as well. We both exclaimed Oh no! This could not be happening to our beautiful little child. We knew that we needed God for a miracle.

Though we were in shock, Dr. Shepherd was excellent. She immediately dispatched an ambulance to send Puffs to Cornell Hospital in New York City because aside from having some of the best doctors, it specialized in treatment and operations on the brain. Dr. Shepherd ordered the nurses to start an I.V. for Puffs while Denie began making calls to family and friends that would pray. Shortly thereafter, Puffs was whisked away in an ambulance headed to Cornell Hospital in New York. Puffs has always had a great sense of humor, and jokingly said, "I've never seen the inside of an ambulance."

Chapter II

The Weapon Song

When we arrived at the hospital Puffs' bed in Room 403 South on the 6th floor was already ready. And we had only been there a short while before we were informed that the doctor wanted Puffs to get a CAT scan. Shortly thereafter, the attendants came and rolled her down the hall to the room she would get the scan in. Throughout the whole time, Puffs was still in good spirits. She was even asking questions like, "What does that mean, CAT scan? I know it doesn't mean they are scanning a cat." We laughed because Puffs has such sense of humor. Denie explained that the CAT scan was going to be used to check out her whole body to see what was causing her so much pain. I thought to myself that Puffs really was a brave little girl lying still for nearly two hours to be tested.

When the attendants had brought Puffs back to the room at 1:30 p.m., I began preparing to leave heading for work. But before I actually left, I wanted to go by the gift store to buy a gift for her. When I returned to the room and was taking the things out of the bag, Denie told me that the doctor had come in to inform her that Puffs was going to have to undergo surgery on her brain to remove the tumor (that had grown there). She said that the operation would take up to 12 hours and was scheduled to take place as quickly as 7:30 the next morning. Puffs was the first patient on the schedule. Before we knew it other family members had already begun arriving and were all shocked, looking at each other in amazement. Everyone seemed frozen, not knowing what to say. But Puffs was still in good spirits. That day no one went home.

Thursday, June 6, 2002

The next day seemed to come very quickly, and before long it was 7:25 a.m.; the attendants were very prompt. They lifted Puffs onto another hospital bed and rolled her down to the operating room. Denie followed along to accompany her daughter. I too was on my way following them when the attendant saw me and said, "Only one is allowed." So instead of protesting, I went back to the room and started straightening it up using my nervous energy. Before I knew it, Denie was standing behind me dressed in a white hat and white suit holding balloons. She said, "They would not let me stay down there for the operation, but Puffs was singing the song when she went in: 'No matter what the weapon is, I want you to know that I win.'" We both hugged each other crying and praying. Puffs had just learned that song a few days before, and it was evident that she was not just singing empty words, but was holding on to those words by faith.

"A little child shall lead them."
Isaiah 11:6

The operation took approximately eight hours. During that time many family and friends came, and to each person we testified that Puffs went in singing the weapon song. After many hours before Puffs arrived back in the room, the doctor came to report that everything had gone well. Puffs hadn't needed any additional blood as was expected, and wasn't dehydrated. However, they did want to keep her and check for bleeding and other things that might occur over the next 24 hours. He said they had gotten everything, but by no means was she out of the woods. When they brought Puffs back to the room she had no tubes in her mouth, was just resting awake at times, and a little groggy from the medication. She was coherent and recognized everybody, praises to God.

"No weapon that is formed against thee shall prosper..."
Isaiah 54:17

Chapter III

It's In the Spirit

Wednesday night was a regular prayer meeting night for my church held in addition to the Bible study where there was a question and answer session. Upon hearing the news of Puffs' emergency surgery my pastor, stopped the prayer meeting to lift up a special prayer for her. He began to explain to the congregation the details of the emergency operation and the seriousness of the brain tumor. Most of the members in the church were already familiar with her because they had known Puffs since the first day she was born. And because Denie used to live close by, my church was the very first church she had taken Puffs to. She had also been a member for about five years herself. Not only had Puffs been christened there, but she had also attended our nursery school. The people at my church were the ones who nicknamed her Puffs. She had a lot of hair and wore those Afro puffs all the time. The Pastor asked the congregation, "If this was your daughter, how would you pray?" Well, everyone prayed that entire evening, strong and powerful for Puffs as never before. I believe as a result of that prayer, Puffs' surgery was successful.

"The effectual fervent prayer of a righteous man availeth much."
James 5:16

Saturday, June 8, 2002

I spent the night at the hospital and prepared to go to church the following Sunday morning while Puffs was still recuperating. But right before I had planned to leave for church Puffs told me she was hungry. We called the nurse and told her to bring Puffs whatever she wanted. When the nurse returned she sat Puffs up in the chair to eat. Puffs first asked for an orange and some applesauce, then she requested some pancakes for breakfast. Once Puffs was done eating, I left heading to church. By the time I had arrived the anointing was so strong that Pastor could not even preach. The Pastor prayed for me and said, "It's in the Spirit; Sis. Ruthie; not by might." She prayed for strength for Puffs and Denie. The Deacon said, "Do not look at the situation, just trust God," he encouraged me by saying, "He can do anything." Many people came up to me and told me they were praying for us. When I had returned to the hospital that afternoon I was pleased to see that Puffs had been moved out of I.C.U into another room 217, 6 north—the power of prayer.

> *"...Not by might, nor by power, but by my spirit,*
> *saith the LORD of hosts."*
> Zechariah 4:6

> *"Trust in the LORD with all thine heart; and lean not unto thine own*
> *understanding. In all thy ways acknowledge him, and he shall direct*
> *thy paths,"*
> Proverbs 3:5-6

Monday, June 10, 2002

I spoke with Denie who was happy to report that, "Puffs walked a little and went to the bathroom with assistance." Praise God! Puffs' dad had also visited and stayed overnight with her. They even played games on the Nintendo system together. That day Puffs had gone to the room where other kids who were staying in the hospital were playing. When

I spoke with her that morning, I said, "I love you Puffs," and she said, "I love you too, Grandma." That evening when I called back I said, "I love you," again. She told me that nothing was hurting her, though she didn't seem happy. She said her dad was outside of the room talking to the nurse, and that she could possibly go home by the end of the week.

Tuesday, June 11, 2002

I received a phone call from someone at the hospital telling me to come right away. I called Denie to find out what was going on and she said, "Puffs has cancer." Even though I heard the words she was saying, I was hoping that what I was hearing was not true. I knew Puffs had been diagnosed with a tumor, but I was hoping it was benign. The dreaded disease of cancer was undeniable: the doctors diagnosed Puffs with a Medulloblastoma tumor. I told Denie that I was on my way. I was still in shock, yet believing God. Because the Pastor had prayed for me only two days prior I could clearly remember her saying, "It's not by might, it's in the spirit Sis. Ruthie." I held on to that word she gave me. I was strengthened to know in ourselves we could do nothing, but through Christ all things were possible. I told myself that I have to trust God, and that there is nothing that God can't handle. He sees all, and knows all. God was present with us. I remembered and kept hearing over and over again Pastor's voice saying, "We believe God. We are not going to waver."

"But let him ask in faith, nothing wavering."
James 1:6

*"Again I say unto you, That if two of you shall agree
on earth, as touching anything that they shall ask,
it shall be done for them of my Father which is in heaven."*
Matthew 18:19

Later that day when I spoke with Denie she told me that the doctors wanted to treat Puffs both with chemotherapy and radiotherapy. They also wanted to transfer her to another facility, but would have to get back to her about the exact location. Denie was disappointed because she thought Puffs was going to be able to go home, so I stayed overnight at the hospital to give Denie extra support. With me staying she was able to go home and prepare Puffs' room, and also get some much needed rest.

CHAPTER IV

Home Again

Wednesday, June 12, 2002

Before leaving for work the next morning, I called my brother in Texas and told him the diagnosis. He in turn called my sister and together they called all the family until everyone had been reached. Immediately an intercessory prayer chain was started for Puffs between family and friends. The Lord let me know that He is Puffs' great physician and that we are to recognize what He is doing, and to remember to esteem Him highly above everything.

> *"...Every knee shall bow to me, and every tongue shall confess to God."*
> Romans 14:11

> *"And God said, Let there be light: and there was light."*
> *(He spoke the world into existence.)*
> Genesis 1:3

After speaking with my brother, I called my aunt because I knew she was a prayer warrior. She said, "Puffs is going to be all right. I am a prayer warrior and I'm going to pray and rebuke the enemy. When the child comes home take her to church and lay her on the altar, just like Hannah did. Puffs is going to be fine."

"And she said, Oh my lord, as thy soul liveth, my lord, I am the woman that stood by thee here, praying unto the LORD. For this child I prayed; and the LORD hath given me my petition which I asked of him: Therefore also I have lent him to the LORD; as long as he liveth he shall be lent to the LORD. And he worshiped the LORD there."

I Samuel 1:26-28

Finally, I called Denie who had been wondering where I had been. I told her that I had been waiting to hear from her. She proceeded to tell me that Puffs was finally going to be discharged, so I took off like a bat and arrived at the hospital to see Puffs, Denie, as well as many other family members. Upon discharge Puffs insisted on being wheeled out in a wheel chair because she knew that when people were discharged from the hospital that they were escorted out this way. We gathered all her balloons, stuffed toys, gifts and bags and went straight to Denie's house.

Thursday, June 13, 2002

I awakened early the next morning at 7 a.m. to pray. I did not have any words to say, so I just lay before God. I kept remembering, "It's in the spirit." I got up and started writing in this book. Instantly I was reminded of the song Denie wrote entitled, "Fear Not," inspired by Isaiah 41:10.

"Fear thou not: For I am with thee; be not dismayed; for I am thy God: I will strengthen thee; yea, I will help thee; yea, I will uphold thee with the right hand of my righteousness."

Isaiah 41:10

CHAPTER V

The Birthday Celebrations

Saturday, June 15, 2002

Saturday was an early morning start for me. Around 1:00 p.m. that afternoon Denie called and sounded very stressed. She said, "Mom please come now." When I called her back to get more information, she said that some of the family was already at her house, and that Puffs was unhappy that day because she hadn't gotten her birthday cake. She reported that Puffs had been very quiet and no one could get her to respond. So the family and friends that were there decided to go out and get her a birthday cake with gifts to celebrate because she had been in the hospital on her actual birthday. Although Puffs received many gifts that included stuffed toys while staying in the hospital, she felt those gifts did not take the place of having a real birthday cake and party. From that incident Puffs taught us all a very valuable lesson.

Then understanding the plans, I quickly hurried to the flea market and was able to find a pretty plastic tray that Puffs could use to eat on while in bed or for doing her homework. The tray was pink, Puffs' favorite color. I thought I even had time to have her name painted on it encircled with flowers. When I finally arrived back to the house, Puffs immediately let me know that I had missed the cutting of her birthday cake. So I quickly cut a piece of her birthday cake and sat down to eat right next to her as she lay on the couch.

The party was made up of good friends and family members and everyone seemed to have had a wonderful time. Puffs definitely seemed much happier, so much so that she began writing a poem. But it wasn't until she began writing this poem that we noticed for the first time that she was not using her right hand to write as she customarily does. We all figured out that her writing hand dominance must have changed as a side effect of the operation. From that point forward Puffs wrote and drew with her left hand. She had always been right-handed, but post operation her right hand had become too weak to manipulate a pencil. As a result, her left hand ended up being much stronger than her right; and she has been left-handed ever since. Everyone was so happy to see that Puffs seemed to be back to her old self. Praise God!

Upon the hospital discharge I made plans to take Denie and Puffs to church with me so she could lay her on the altar as my aunt suggested. However, because Denie was having so many sleepless nights trying to make Puffs more comfortable, she was at her wits end. Contrary to Denie's wishes, the doctors prescribed steroids for Puffs to take as part of her recovery treatment. In view of that, one night after following the doctor's orders, Denie had given Puffs her daily dosage of steroids when suddenly Puffs' heart began to race abnormally fast. To say the least, this was a very frightening experience for Denie. She prayed and by faith made a wise decision to discontinue the treatment of steroids.

One day I had stopped by to see Puffs and she was complaining that her head, heart, gums, right leg, and neck were numb. So, before we went home, we all joined in prayer for Puffs.

> *"A merry heart doeth good like a medicine:*
> *but a broken spirit driest the bones."*
> Proverbs 17:22

Sunday, June 16, 2002

The following day happened to be Sunday, so I went to church. Immediately following service, the Pastor asked to see me in her office. She shared with me that she was very concerned about Puffs' condition. I proceeded to bring her up to date and I told her that Puffs wanted to come to our church. She told me to have Denie do what Puffs wanted her to do; so when I went home I called Denie. At first there was no answer, then finally she picked up the phone. Denie explained that Puffs was in her dad's backyard because they were having a cookout in her honor as part of her birthday celebration and homecoming party.

"Like as a father pitieth his children, so the LORD pitieth them that hear him."
Psalms 103:13

CHAPTER VI

God Is In Control

Monday, June 17, 2002

On Monday morning Puffs was scheduled to go to the hospital to see the doctor at 10 a.m., but Denie called ahead to the nurse's station to tell them we would be a little bit late. When we arrived at 10:30 a.m. the doctor took Denie aside and spoke with her. Denie later shared with me that the doctor was leaning towards placing Puffs into another facility. The whole time the doctor was talking to Denie, Puffs sat and drew pictures. Shortly after the doctor finished speaking with Denie, he removed the stitches from the back of Puffs' head. She was very brave and did not cry.

For a change in atmosphere, Denie decided to come home with me for a few days. She took my car to pick up clothes for herself and Puff, then we all headed straight for my church. There, Denie, Puffs and I lay on the altar and prayed. After we finished praying, Denie requested that she go alone to a park. She stayed there from 4 p.m. until 7 p.m. After I picked her up from the park we went home and ate dinner.

"...but the Spirit itself maketh intercession for us with groanings which cannot be uttered. And he that searcheth

the hearts knoweth what is the mind of the Spirit, because
he maketh intercession for the saints according to the will of God."
Romans 8:26-27

Tuesday, June 18, 2002

A friend called Denie to let her know that she was interceding in prayer on behalf of Puffs. She went on to say that one day while she was watching a TV ministry, the televangelist announced that, "I see a little girl with a brain tumor being healed right now." Denie's friend said that she instantly laid her hands on the television screen in agreement with the word of the Lord. Denie was excited and confirmed her agreement with the word. She also reported that she was thanking God because Puffs' swelling had gone since she had stopped giving her the steroids.

Wednesday, June 19, 2002

Today I took Denie to visit with her cousin who lived in Brentwood, New York. Brentwood was about a 25-minute ride from where I lived. After the early afternoon visit, her cousin drove Denie back home to Jamaica, NY, which was about a 45-minute ride. In the meantime I tried to call Denie a few times while she was away, but the phone dumped me right into the voicemail each time. It finally dawned on me that Denie must have had so many messages on her phone that it could not hold anymore. So I just waited for her to return.

Thursday, June 20, 2002

The next day I didn't actually see Denie, but she did call to let me know that the human resources office at her job was making contact with the doctors in order for Puffs to be treated. They wanted to make sure she was receiving the best care and had the best doctors. In the meantime, she had received a call from some officials of Saint Jude's Hospital located in Tennessee explaining the details of their eight-month program they wanted to offer Puffs. As a benefit of the program Denie and Puffs would both fly free of cost. Their lodging would be free as well as all of their expenses would be paid. The representative further explained that Denie's insurance company would not even so much as receive a bill. She was further informed about Saint Jude's follow-up program that continues throughout the child's entire life, as opposed to the five-week program offered in New York that consisted of two days of chemotherapy with three days of radiation. We began praying along those lines, and Denie started researching every avenue as to which direction she should take.

Saturday, June 22, 2002

I had been trying to reach Denie, but her phone was constantly busy. When she finally did pick up she said, "Mom I haven't been answering the phone because I've been trying to get some rest. The Lord gave me a song in my spirit, so I got on my keyboard and was playing the tune all night and I'm tired." She said, "This praise song just came out of my spirit: He that dwelleth in the secret place of the Most High shall abide under the shadow of the Almighty. I will say of the LORD. He is my refuge and my fortress: my God; in him will I trust." Psalm 91:1-2

Sunday, June 23, 2002

The next day I spoke to her briefly and was happy to hear that she had rested most of the day while Puffs had gone to a recital with her grandmother on her father's side. She told me that she was just leaving to pick Puffs up, and that hopefully Puffs will catch up on her rest when she gets home.

Tuesday, June 25, 2002

Denie and Puffs went to 6 a.m. prayer.

Wednesday, June 26, 2002

Puffs had a doctor's appointment at 12:30. When I made it to Denie's house at 11:05, she began to explain that she had just spoken to someone from the hospital who informed her that merely having a consultation would cost her $525.00. She immediately called her insurance company only to find out the bad news, these services would not be covered. Needless to say Denie was very upset, and just cancelled the appointment. I didn't understand how they could charge her so much when she needed the information on what and how they were going to treat Puffs.

But before we could even get out of the house, a friend called and had a doctor on the line who could possibly help Denie. The doctor was an undercover Afro-American naturopathic doctor who believes you can fight any disease by altering your current dietary plan. Denie was on the phone for about 30 minutes with this doctor who suggested that they set up a special diet for Puffs.

Because of this wonderful phone call, we were able to start making plans for Denie and Puffs to attend the mother and daughter tea being sponsored by my church instead of going to the hospital. We had gotten so excited about our plans that Denie suggested we head to Brooklyn to go shopping. All of us got in the car headed toward the FDR Drive and went to downtown Brooklyn. We parked the car in Macy's parking garage, but quickly realized we were all hungry, especially Puffs, and started looking for a place to eat first. We noticed that there was a restaurant called Juniors that we had never dined in before. We decided to have lunch there and were seated pretty quickly. It ended up being a great lunch. Of course we didn't leave without taking a doggie bag, which included cheesecake topped with strawberries. By the time we finished eating it was too late to go shopping; so I took Denie and Puffs home. While on the way to her house Denie told me about an easy way to avoid the evening rush hour I would inevitably run into on my return home. She said although I would have a bunch more lights, I would still end up saving a lot of time. So I dropped the two of them off and drove her suggested route home.

Friday, June 28, 2002

I spoke to Denie and found out that she and one of her friends had gone to noonday prayer. That day the ministers just happened to be teaching from a scripture on healing. Denie received a word from the Lord that said, "God has got the situation under control. Trust in Him. He is molding and shaping you in the midst of this. He just wants you to trust Him."

Later that day while on her way home from prayer, Denie stopped off at a dress shop and ran into another friend she hadn't seen in a long time. She immediately greeted both Denie and Puffs with a long embrace. She and Denie caught up on the events that had taken place since they had last seen each other and ended up riding the Q4 bus home together. When it was time for her friend to get off the bus, Puffs began whining to Denie that she wanted to go to the friend's house because she was not yet ready to go home. Denie decided that since they would be passing right by Puffs' school, that maybe it would be a good idea to pay her teacher and classmates a visit instead. So they got off the bus right in front of Puffs' school and went to visit. Puffs had been very fortunate to be able to attend a Christian school. When they saw Puffs' teacher, she greeted them both and gave Puffs a big hug. She told her that the entire school had been praying for her and that they all missed her so much. Puffs' classmates presented her with a checker game as a gift, and Puffs' best friend gave her a big hug and a card.

The principal wanted Denie and Puffs to go back to his office where he talked, prayed, and anointed Puffs. He said Elijah came to his spirit as he wrapped his arms around Puffs and anointed her head with oil.

> *"And there appeared unto them Elijah with Moses: and they were talking with Jesus. And Peter answered and said to Jesus, Master, it is good for us to be here..."*
> Mark 9:4-5

After leaving the school, Denie decided to visit another friend, who happened to live close to the school. Her friend had gone shopping but planned to be home by the time Denie arrived: this did not happen. Her friend was still shopping when Denie and Puffs arrived because she happened to be one of those shoppers that shop until they drop. So Denie called her cell phone and she said she would be there within minutes. Denie had already called me to pick her and Puffs up because we had also planned to spend some time together at my house. I actually made it to the friend's house before she did, so Denie and Puffs waited in my car for her. That evening it was a bit cold, though not freezing, but Denie assured me that her friend was indeed on the way. We had only been waiting a brief moment before the friend drove up. The friend kept saying how happy she was that she had taken Denie to prayer with her, and that she had started crying when the preacher began speaking on healing. She said that she was trying to go back to prayer that Thursday, but it didn't work out in her schedule. I reassured her that everything happened all in God's timing. We noticed that Puffs must have been worn out from the day's activities because she was knocked out and slept until 8:25 a.m. the next morning. That morning Denie awakened with a song called "Arise" in her spirit and was playing my keyboard when I got up for prayer. When she and I started talking, she reminded me about how the principal had anointed Puffs at her school.

Chapter VII

Puffs' Name Changed to "Miracle"

Saturday, June 29, 2002

Denie and Puffs spent the night with me because the mother daughter tea was being held that weekend at my church. When we all got up we ate breakfast and rushed to pick up pink dresses before noon because all of the attendees were asked to wear pink. We left going to the church at about 11:00 a.m., but Denie said she wanted to stop by the mall on the way. We were able to find a dress for Puffs at the first store we went to, and in another store found dresses on sale just alike for ourselves. We were so happy that by noon we had already paid for the dresses; and by 12:40 we were arriving at the church.

The program at the tea was well underway when the announcement was made for everyone to look under their chairs for a white dot to indicate the winner of the door prize. And by design, Puffs looked under her chair and found the white dot. When she went up to claim her prize, the emcee asked her about her healing. So to help her share it, Puffs asked for her mother to come and give the miracle testimony of the operation.

Later in the service Puffs had started feeling itchy, so I asked her if she wanted to go up for prayer. She said that she did, but wanted both Denie and I to go with her. While in the front of the room, the guest speaker, who happened to be a prophet, began prophesying healing to Puffs and a new level of anointing. She said that, "She will preach, prophesy and dance like David." She also said that her name, just like Sarai's name was changed to Sarah, would be changed to Miracle. She also proclaimed that there would be no reoccurrence of the cancer. The prophet declared that Puffs was going to live to preach God's word. I was hoping we could remain until the end, but Denie had scheduled for the nurse physiotherapist to come to the house at 3 p.m. that day.

"And God said unto Abraham, As for Sarai thy wife; thou shalt not call her name Sarai, but Sarah shall her name be."

Genesis 17:15

Sunday, June 30, 2002

Now it was the last day of June, about three weeks from Puffs' operation. When I spoke to Denie, she told me that she had plans to go to dinner, and that earlier that morning she had gone to church and shared her testimony. She went on to say that the church service was highly anointed. We talked about how most people don't survive when they have a tumor the size of a peach like Puffs has, and how much of a miracle she really was. I told her that I had also gone to church and was blessed by the services, and that someone had left a beautiful china doll on my chair as a gift for Puffs. I also shared with Denie that camp meeting services were starting that week and that the dancers may possibly minister that song "No Weapon." I told her that the dancers were hoping Puffs could be in service that day. Denie thought the idea was really nice, but didn't think they would be able to make it. The dancers decided to wait to minister the song at another time when Puffs could be in service.

Chapter VIII

Prizes and Surprises

Saturday, July 6, 2002

We had planned for Puffs to spend the weekend with her grandparents in Long Island because I thought it was time to have a Grandma's Day. Denie told me that Puffs was at her cousin's house in Huntington, so I called her and made arrangements to pick her up from there. When I arrived at her house at 10:15 a.m., Puffs' hair was combed in such a pretty updo that revealed the scar from the operation. Puffs seemed to be quite happy with wearing her hair pinned up.

When we got in the car we decided to go to Macy's to shop for a couple of dresses, but I immediately remembered that I needed to stop at an ATM first. Luckily Puffs knew exactly where one was located for the sake of not wasting time, and led me back to the entrance door of the store. Sure enough there was the ATM; and funny that I hadn't even noticed it when I walked through the door. I said thanks to Puffs while she watched me take money from the ATM. I could see she was curious to know how much money I was getting out of the machine.

We took the escalator to the second floor and found some very pretty dresses: one was red and white; the other was a pink floral dress with hints of lavender in it. She also got a few other things that little girls like, but Puffs was rushing me because she wanted to hurry on to our next stop: Adventure Land.

So we left Macy's headed to Adventure Land, and to my surprise Puffs wanted me to go on all the rides with her. We rode on the Tube on Water, the Lady Bug, the Train, and drove the cars. We had so much fun; we even won a couple of gifts. We left Adventure Land going home, was going to stop to pick up some shoes, but Puffs was so sleepy she could not go in the store. Puffs was still knocked out when we got home, but when she woke up she kept saying, "I want my mommy. I want my mommy." She was sad and crying. She told me that she didn't ever have to sleep by herself because her mom was always there. I told her that I would sleep with her that night. She didn't complain anymore.

Sunday, July 7, 2002

I made breakfast and prepared to leave for Sunday school at 8:30 a.m. At church Puffs sat next to her grandpa, but seemed a little lonely. So I called her over to the keyboard to help me play, and that seemed to make her happy. That day the dance ministry danced especially for Puffs: "No Matter What the Weapon is I want you to know that I win." Puffs looked on in amazement. It had been such a blessing that the Pastor had them do it again. After service Pastor hugged Puffs and prayed for her. Many people were happy to see her.

"...The Lord hath done great things for us; whereof we are glad."
Psalm 126:3

CHAPTER IX

The New Doctor

Monday, July 8, 2002

Monday morning Denie called the new doctor, a friend of the family recommended to her, and set up an appointment for Thursday at 1 p.m.

Wednesday, July 10, 2002

The doctor left a message on my answering machine and called me on my cell phone. She was looking forward to meeting with Denie and Puffs. She wanted to know Puffs' favorite color and what fruits she liked to eat. I told her Puffs' favorite color was pink and that she liked oranges and apples. She said, "I'm getting something together because I like to do something special for the little ones that come. Please don't tell Puffs, though you can tell her mom." She asked how to correctly pronounce Puffs' name. She had also been mispronouncing Denie's name, and was calling her Deleine so I politely corrected her and let her know the correct pronunciation. She quickly apologized for the error and said Denie's name was hard to read on the fax she had received. When Denie and I spoke she let me know that she had faxed me the directions on how to get to the doctor though I wasn't able to read it because my fax machine was low on ink. She told me that I would have to leave as early as I could if I wanted to accompany them on their trip to New Jersey to see the doctor.

Thursday, July 11, 2002

It was 7:35 a.m., and I had been up since 6:05 a.m. praying and reading scriptures. Puffs reminded me on the phone the night before that I told her I would bring a goody bag for her, so I packed a cooler full of fruit for her. When I picked Denie up at 10:30 a.m. Puffs came out of the house with a big white teddy bear with red ears. She was in good spirits wearing a floral pink, white, green, and orange dress with her hair in two ponytails in front and one in the back. After Denie came down we all stopped off at McDonald's for breakfast. Puffs had begun to cry because she wanted the same food as Denie who was eating right in front of her. After a while Puffs stopped crying and opened her goody bag and ate two plums, some grapes, an apple, some kiwi, strawberries and a mango.

We arrived at the doctor's office by 12:30 p.m. and waited in the car until 1:05 p.m. before heading up to suite 208. When we entered the building we noticed a pink balloon with a big pink card and Puffs' name written on it. We opened the door to see that all the way up the stairs were pink balloons. Puffs couldn't help smiling. We were introduced to the doctor, and she seemed overjoyed to meet us. We were in her office until about 5:30 that evening being taught how to combine foods. The doctor humbly admitted that she can't heal or cure anyone, but taught us that when the immune system is in tact it heals the body itself. We learned so much about the body and how to feed it that day.

Saturday, July 13, 2002

That day happened to be hot, so I spent some time cleaning the yard and my flowerbeds. At the end of the day I went shopping at the health food store because by the time we were done visiting with the doctor all of our eating habits had been changed.

Sunday, July 14, 2002

This was a day of prayer. Puffs' great-grandmother, Susan E. Griffin born in 1908, had she lived would have been celebrating her 94th birthday on that day. Puffs had the honor of being held by her great-grandmother Susan when she was a tiny baby, and still had the pretty pink and white nylon dress she gave her when she was born.

On that day my sister, had been involved in a very bad car accident where she totaled the car; but through prayer, she survived it. Thank God. Also on that day I found out that my Pastor had been admitted into the hospital. We had a special prayer of agreement for healing.

Thursday, July 18, 2002

Denie wanted to go shopping and look for a juicing machine for Puffs. She was able to find one that was only priced at $89.00. Unfortunately neither one of us could afford to buy the juicer at that time, so Denie decided she would pick it up when she was better able to pay for it.

Monday, July 22, 2002

On this night Denie called me telling me that she had to sign for a package that was sent from her job. I immediately began to wonder if everything was all right. She told me that when she opened it she found $3,000 dollars in it. She had become so excited because she realized people from everywhere had sent her checks. She said there was even a check for $200.00 from her own boss. I was shocked to hear how these people were being lead to give without Denie even having to ask them for donations; they just felt to give. So she was lifted in her spirit. Denie also told me how three weeks prior she had felt so strongly in her spirit to sow into a certain ministry, and now knew the importance of sowing.

"Give, and it shall be given unto you; good measure, pressed down and shaken together, and running over, shall men give into your bosom. For with the same measure that ye mete withal it shall be measured to you again."
Luke 6:38

Tuesday July 23, 2002

Denie called twice that day, once in the morning and once in the evening excited about finding a sale at a store that was going out of business. She found shorts for $3 and dresses for $10. She bought Puffs and herself three outfits a piece. Her voice sounded like she was the old Denie again. When she called that evening she said Puffs was singing "We Shall Overcome" with rifts in her voice; she was happy. Denie and Puffs continued doing fun things.

Thursday, July 25, 2002

Denie received a book from her doctor called "Proto-call" which outlined and described the types of vitamins Puffs would need to take. The doctor told Denie it was imperative for her to read the book; as well as gave her the do's and don'ts about combining food. The doctor also gave Denie some vitamins that would help to detoxify Puffs' body. The book had quite a few pages written by the doctor that dealt specifically with Puffs' condition.

Thursday, August 1, 2002

August had come, and there were so many financial matters Denie still needed to get straightened out. As a result of not bringing in an income she hadn't been able to do anything about her bills. But all thanks goes to God for providing a resource of money she could use to help her get on her feet again, and soon have her car on the road.

Thursday, August 08, 2002

I boarded a Delta airlines' flight at 5 a.m. in the morning to catch my connecting flight to Dallas Fort worth, Texas to my family reunion. When I arrived everyone was asking about Puffs' health and I was so happy to tell them about the miracle and that she had been doing well. Many mentioned that they had been praying for Puffs every day. I reminded them of how awesome God is and encouraged them to please continue praying for her.

Now a few days had passed since arriving home from my short vacation and I was anxious to see both Denie and Puffs. I arranged to pick Puffs up so that we could spend the day at Sunken Meadow beach. We slipped our bathing suits on, and we were off to have lots of fun. On the next day Puffs wanted to go to Chuck E Cheese, so Grandpa and I took her, and there we had so much fun riding on lots of rides, laughing and playing.

Monday, September 2, 2002

Labor Day arrived and Denie decided to have a victory party in honor of Puffs at Jillian's Entertainment Center. A few family members and friends came together to celebrate with us. When I spoke with Denie she informed me that Puffs had gone back to school and was doing very well, even doing her homework all by herself.

Saturday, September 21, 2002

Two weeks later I had the privilege of taking Denie shopping at Western Beef's located in Queens. When we arrived to the store, Puffs immediately jumped in my wagon to be pushed around. She brought along her doll that I had given her at the victory party that laughs, cries, drinks from a bottle and opens and closes her eyes. Puffs liked to treat the doll as if she were a real baby and kept real diapers on her. While at the store we put some fresh batteries in the back of the doll, and Puffs was a happy girl. Overall she had been doing a lot better though her new challenge had become drinking all of her health drink every morning because it was very thick. Along with the health drink she had to take three or four huge vitamin pills. In my opinion the pills should have been cut in half and she would still get the nutrients she needed. But because Puffs wanted to stay well she drank and swallowed the pills the best she could.

Wednesday, December 11, 2002

Two months had passed and the time had come for Denie to take Puffs to have her blood tested for any traces of cancer. On that day the report had come back that the only thing Puffs had was a urinary infection and was slightly anemic. Praise God! God can't lie. She was healed of cancer. Puffs' name had indeed been changed to "Miracle".

Chapter X

Another Miracle

Saturday, December 28, 2002

A little over two weeks later Denie called saying that she wanted to spend the night out and was going to come straight out to my house. I persuaded her to go home first to get what she needed for herself and Puffs. We made plans to meet at my church. She agreed that was a better idea and went home to pick up what she needed and met me at my church. When we arrived to my house she discovered that Puffs' medication was not with her. She was hoping that she hadn't left it on the train, so she put in a call to the railroad office, but to no avail. She called the taxi company, no bag was found. She called to check if someone at the church had noticed it, to no avail. No bag of medication was found. In the meantime, Denie explained to me that the vitamin supplements were very expensive and she hated having to call and reorder them. She had also been making sure she fed Puffs veggies, greens, and other vitamins to further supplement her diet.

"He that dwelleth in the secret place of the Most High shall abide under the shadow of the Almighty. I will say of the LORD, He is my refuge and my fortress: my God; in him will I trust."

Psalm 91:1-2

Saturday, January 25, 2003

On this day Puffs had begun complaining of headaches again, though she did go to a youth meeting that evening. Two days later Puffs had gone with her mother and father to church, but was still complaining of her head aching. The following Monday, Puffs had gone to school yet still complaining of headaches. I reminded Denie that Puffs' health was very important and that she needed to see the doctor right away. So the next day when Puffs came home complaining that her head was hurting and the words seemed to be jumping off the blackboard, Denie took her to the emergency room immediately.

By the time that I made it to Jamaica Hospital, Denie and a friend of hers had been waiting in the emergency care unit about five hours. They had taken X-rays and done an MRI and determined that something was there. Immediately the staff began making preparations for Puffs to be taken by ambulance to Cornell University New York Presbyterian Hospital. In the meantime we were praying that the cancer had not returned. After we arrived at the hospital in the city more X-rays were done and it was determined that indeed it was a reoccurrence of the cancer. We immediately called the Pastor for prayer.

Wednesday, January 29, 2003

The doctors planned the second surgery, and upon examination found Puffs to be very alert. Puffs went into surgery at 1 p.m. and did not return until 7 p.m. when finally the doctor came to the waiting room to tell us the surgery had been successful. The surgical staff reported that they had gotten about 98% of the cancer with the other 2% being in the brain stem. Twenty-four hours later Puffs had a follow-up MRI with the doctor reporting that the results were very good.

Friday, January 31, 2003

Today, Puffs was recuperating and had only slight headaches.

Saturday, February 1, 2003

Puffs had no more headaches and she seemed to be very alert. By this time Puffs was standing up, walking, talking and even eating her dinner, which consisted of string beans, macaroni and cheese, and juice. Puffs is God's little miracle.

Prior to this day a sister from my church told me about a dream she had where God said another miracle was coming. I wholeheartedly believed this successful second surgery was the miracle she was talking about. That day was the day Puffs was being moved out of ICU into a regular room.

Sunday, February 2, 2003

I did not go to the hospital that Sunday afternoon, but instead went to service at my church. However after service I went straight to the city to spend the night at the hospital with Puffs. When I arrived I told Denie to take my car so she could take care of what she needed to do. Denie didn't return until around 2:30 the next afternoon. While she was gone I was enjoying my time playing with Puffs who had drawn two pictures and even had gone to play in the playroom. Once I left the hospital, the doctor released Puffs to go home.

Tuesday, February 4, 2003

A couple days later Denie called to tell me that she hadn't been sleeping well and had been crying. I tried to encourage her by telling her that the enemy wanted her to be fearful and reminded her that we couldn't operate by fear, but by faith. I proceeded to tell the devil that he was a liar and prayed for her. Later she told me a friend had called and really was a help to her as well that day.

Wednesday, February 5, 2003

Denie started getting things set up with the Social Security department, and the Cancer Society, and discovered that through her job she was entitled to an additional medical benefit also. As a result she set up an appointment with the cancer doctor for chemo & radiotherapy, for February 11 at 11 a.m., and would be going to a counselor on that Thursday. Before I left them, Puffs reminded me to not forget to bring along the cooler because it was packed with goodies of fruit.

Tuesday, February 11, 2003

Puffs' appointment was with the doctor at Sloan Kettering, located directly across the street from the New York Presbyterian Hospital. Even though we were late for Puffs' appointment, they did examine her quite a few times. She had to touch her toes, push with her feet and squeeze with her hands as part of these preliminary tests. Later, when Denie finally spoke with the doctor, he reported that Puffs was in good shape. The team of doctors began to share with us the follow-up plan they made for Puffs and explained how they rate certain parts as being high or low. If the ratings were high Puffs would more than likely have to have another operation. Puffs had a high rating, which brought down the factor of more chemo or less chemo versus another week or two with radiology. They thought it best to prepare for another operation because of the 2% of cancer that remained in her body. They determined that if they could remove some of the cancer she could opt for less chemo and radiology. Denie did not want Puffs to have chemo because of the side effects on the thyroid, possible hearing loss, eye damage, growth stunting, liver damage, sterility, hair loss as well as a 10% chance of developing cancer again. It was said that Puffs could also be in need of blood transfusions in the future as a result of chemotherapy.

The doctor added that he would never treat Puffs again if Denie declined chemo and refused to follow the treatment he prescribed for her. But because Denie was solely on a higher spiritual level, she didn't seem to let anything he said bother her. Praise God. Everything was being put before the Lord.

> *"For verily I say unto you, That whosoever shall say unto this mountain, Be thou removed, and be thou cast into the sea; and shall not doubt in his heart, but shall believe that those things which he saith shall come to pass; he shall have whatsoever he saith."*
>
> Mark 11:23

Denie scheduled a follow-up appointment for that Friday to get everything finalized because the doctors wanted to operate on Monday, February 17, 2003. Puffs appeared normal upon sight, and had been a real trooper; she complied with everything they asked her to do. Everyone was praying and believing God for the third operation, and yet another miracle.

Monday, February 17, 2003

When Monday arrived Denie was supposed to take Puffs for a procedure to insert a med port line for medication. This procedure was supposed to make it easier to administer medication without having to stick Puffs so much. Instead we had a bad snowstorm that the newscasters coined, "the perfect snowstorm". Why they called it that? I don't know, for us it was horrible. No one was going anywhere.

When I called Denie she told me that the MRI results came back showing no cancer down the spine, but the doctors still wanted to do a spinal tap. Denie was worried about the radiation they would use on the spine because it could have permanent sterility effects. So she rescheduled the appointment.

Wednesday, February 26, 2003

Puffs was taken to Sloan Kettering to have the med port put in. She stayed overnight because the third operation was scheduled early the next morning at 7:30 a.m. and was supposed to take seven hours.

When I arrived to the facility at about 8 a.m. that morning Puffs was in the recovery room so fast that I thought something bad had happened. The operation had only taken four hours. One of the doctors reported that the operation was easy and everything had gone well. Puffs had remained in the hospital until that Saturday and had been moved from room M12 to M25 to M24 on the 5th floor, and finally discharged home.

Sunday, March 2, 2003

When I had spoken to Denie at 11:30 p.m. she said that she had gone out to dinner and had a real spread. She also told me that some of her friends had bought Puffs some red slippers as a gift and she absolutely loved them.

Friday, March 7, 2003

Puffs had another appointment scheduled, and had to be at the hospital by 10:30 a.m. Because it had been extremely cold when it snowed on Thursday the snow had frozen into sheets of ice on the street. As a result, traffic was crawling along at 20 miles an hour. I kept calling Denie and was praying that I could get them to the hospital on time. When I finally made it to Denie's house she and Puffs were downstairs, ready to get in the car. We arrived to the hospital at 10:27 by my clock in the car, and as soon as we stepped in Puffs' name was called to check her weight and blood pressure. At about 1 p.m. she was first called for the simulator, which takes a picture to pinpoint where to use the radiology equipment. Because they thought the procedure would take two hours, Denie and I went out front to wait for her. We soon heard our names being called because Puffs had gone to recovery after only being gone one hour. They made black marks on her skin with a little marker. When Puffs woke up Denie had to calm her down because she was crying and cold. She was also hungry because she hadn't had anything to eat since 12 midnight the night before. We hurried to get her some lunch and took it with us.

The following week Puffs spent some time with her father's mother. So while she was gone, Denie cleaned the house, put up some blinds in her room, straightened Puffs' room, and even went through some bags of clothing not being worn. To say the least, Denie used her time wisely because on March 17, Puffs was scheduled to start cancer treatments.

Sunday, March 9,2003 – Sunday, March 16, 2003

I didn't see Denie this week, and we only spoke on the phone.

Monday 17, 2003

We arrived on time for Puffs' 10:30 a.m. appointment. We parked the car and went to the pediatrics unit located on the third floor. While we were there the doctor inserted a med port into Puffs' chest for administering medications, and for easy access to her blood.

Throughout this entire process Puffs maintained her faith. While on the way to the appointment I had forgotten to mention that I had brought along a clear bottle of blessed oil, the size of a nail polish jar. I had used it many times before to anoint Puffs. But when she saw it she grabbed it like it was gold, so I anointed her right then and prayed for her. I'm happy to report that Puffs anoints herself everyday.

That day happened to be the first day Puffs was ever hooked up to an I.V. on a pole that rolls and with a bag attached. First they checked her height and weight, then we waited. When her name was finally called she was to be given radiation & chemotherapy (Vin Kristin-semi chemo). The first radiation took longer than normal and she came out disoriented and a little whiney, but after a while was okay. She also seemed very tired from the Vin Kristin and was so knocked out that Denie had to get a wheelchair to take her downstairs to put her in the car.

On the way home Puffs woke up and started complaining about nausea so I stopped the car. She opened the back door and proceeded to throw up; we immediately took her home. Later Denie told me Puffs had been up and down all night vomiting some green stuff, but did make it through the night. In the morning Denie called the hospital and the staff gave her a schedule of appointments for the rest of the week.

Tuesday, March 18, 2003

The next morning the doctor wanted Puffs to have 20 minutes of radiation. When they arrived, Denie immediately began to share with him about the things that had been happening with Puffs. He had been unaware that Puffs had been receiving rounds of Vin Kristin. This news made Denie very upset and told him that she expected all of Puffs' doctors to be on the same page. The doctor prescribed medication for Puffs to take every 12 hours to help with the vomiting symptoms she was having, and he and Denie discussed that Puffs would have six weeks of radiology. At that time Puffs was considered a high risk because of the Medulloblastoma cancer tumor that had been removed.

Thursday, March 20, 2003

Puffs had another appointment at Sloan Kettering scheduled at 3:55 p.m., and Denie was able to get it moved up to 3 p.m. When we arrived at 3:30 I dropped them off at the side entrance where the A elevators were located, and went to park the car. Denie told me when I returned to use the side entrance and go pass the A elevator to another set of elevators— I remembered none of that. Instead I went up to the second floor and saw a lady who gave me directions, but did not realize that she was actually sending me to Puffs' 5:30 MRI appointment. So of course Puffs was not there. I did end up finding her though, but in the meantime I began working on a report I had brought with me so that I could finish some work for my job. Before I could even finish, Puffs was back out in the lobby just like a spring chicken. She seemed to be feeling good because Denie had been giving her a vitamin mix that gave her lots of energy.

When we left and picked up the car about 7:00 p.m., Puffs mentioned that she wanted to go to Red Lobster's; so we headed to Green Acres Mall where Red Lobster's was located. When we arrived there was a 30-minute wait because it was crowded. Once we ate, we realized the lobster and shrimp scampi was well worth the wait because dinner was Denie's treat.

A few days had passed before I had spoken with Denie again and when we talked I discovered all was well. She had taken Puffs with her to her church and said the guest minister had delivered a very relevant message. She also let me know that her church held Bible study on Wednesdays and that she wanted to go. I had spoken with Denie on the next morning and found her so excited about the Lord giving her a beautiful song in her spirit. She began to play and sing for me right there on the phone. Some of the melodies seemed like sounds of heaven. In this same conversation, she told me that she had let Puffs comb her own hair.

Another Tuesday had come and Puffs was scheduled for her 20-minute radiology treatment. While in treatments, Puffs had also started attending school at the hospital and had gotten homework from her teacher. Upon leaving the hospital Puffs said that she wanted to go to Central Park, so I dropped her and Denie off to spend some quality time together at the park.

Wednesday, March 26, 2003

I picked Denie and Puffs up early. Puffs appeared to be very tired, but once she had been awake for a while and had arrived at the hospital she seemed to be okay. Denie and Puffs decided to have breakfast first before going to the treatment area. While they were in the cafeteria the nurse had come to look for them a couple of times. Denie and Puffs finally decided to leave the cafeteria so that Puffs could go to class as well as be given her Vin Kristin treatment. While in treatment, the nursing staff also checked her blood count. Before I had gone home I stopped Denie by the store to pick up a prescription for a 12-hour medication that was supposed to help Puffs keep her food down. After we left the store I drove Denie and Puffs home; Puffs seemed tired but functioning. Later that night Denie received a call from the hospital staff informing her that Puffs' blood count was down, but that was to be expected.

Thursday, March 27, 2003

When I spoke with Denie after she had taken Puffs to the hospital, she told me that Puffs was doing fine; and that they had been given tickets to attend the Barnum & Bailey Circus that coming Friday. They decided they would go right after Puffs' had gotten her round of treatments.

Sunday, March 30, 2003

Sunday is the Lord's day, and the Apostle gave us insight on how to let our spirit get to a higher level. He had had a vision of a huge wall of water coming to shore wiping out tents, houses, and everything. The Pastor confirmed that she had also saw the water in the church. Both of them instructed us to get into God and learn how to get our spirit to a higher level. The word of the Lord was true because two years later on August 29, 2005 Hurricane Katrina hit New Orleans, and thousands of homes were wiped out and everything.

Monday, March 31, 2003

Denie took Puffs to the hospital and returned home. She told me that a room was reserved for Puffs at the Ronald McDonald House, and that she would need to use my car to go to the Social Security Office. She also told me that she had to get to the hospital because they were planning to take an X-ray of Puffs' head in sections preparing to radiate the brain for two and half weeks. She said that it would take a little longer than usual.

I arrived at Denie's house early for her to drive to the Social Security office and return by 11:00. Because she had already packed their bags for their stay at the Ronald McDonald House, once she returned home we were able to immediately take off heading for the city. Once there we dropped the clothing bags in her room 1001. Puffs' had a big room that was adorned with a picture window, T.V., VCR, large bed, couch, bathtub and shower. Puffs was so happy, and Denie was very pleased. After looking at Puffs' accommodations, I then drove them to Sloan Kettering, which was just in walking distance.

When I spoke to Denie later she said Puffs had noticed that her hair had begun to fall out and had started to cry a little bit. Denie told her not to cry and reassured her that losing her hair was a small price to pay for her life. She said Puffs didn't cry long and seemed to be all right after she encouraged her. Puffs was still making a practice of daily using the anointing oil that I had given her, and anointing herself in the name of Jesus.

Denie and Puffs enjoyed their first of six weeks at the McDonald House. I picked them up their first Friday there and brought them back to Jamaica Queens for the weekend. Puffs told me that at the McDonald House the staff played with all the patients, and that self-esteem building activities were built into their program for all the children too. She also told me that instead of driving, she and her mom would walk to their appointments for chemo and radiation since Sloan Kettering was located down the street. Once they were settled in, I gave Puffs a bath and helped her put her clothes on. Afterwards I cut a fresh apple and poured some orange juice for her to enjoy while she watched T.V. and braided her dolls hair into long little braids. Denie didn't even know she could braid like that until I told her.

Someone had given Puffs some more tickets to the circus, so the next day she and Denie went and had a good time. When they came back Puffs told me that at the end of the show Kirk Franklin's music was played. I was also excited to hear that she and Denie had the chance to see one of the actors from the show "Everybody Loves Raymond" who was there at the Ronald McDonald House visiting with Fox News. Oftentimes throughout that process people would shower them with love and give Puffs gifts, which really helped to lift her spirit at crucial times. Denie said that it was an experience of a lifetime.

"But my God shall supply all your need
according to his riches in glory by Christ Jesus."
Philippians 4:19

Chapter XI

The Faith Trip to Texas

Once the treatments were completed a good friend, who was into health products big time, helped Denie find a holistic doctor. This friend was very instrumental in helping to locate a doctor in Texas, online. Even though Denie had received offers to take Puffs other places she said, "I prayed and asked God to direct my path and things just seemed to work out well," when she finally made the decision to go to Texas where the doctor was located. Puffs' treatment machine, which consisted of vitamins, oxygen, and another special machine was supposed to cost $1,000 per week.

As God directed her Denie planned the trip to Texas for September. God greatly blessed her to receive donations from many of the churches she had sang in over the years as well as the financial support from the people on her job. Even the human resources representative felt compelled to take up a collection. Everyone just gave from his or her heart. There were many people that Denie did not even know whose hearts were touched by God to give.

I had accompanied Denie on her trip to Texas, and while we were waiting to board the plane the flight attendant upgraded us to first class seats. God was just so awesome. Upon our arrival we stayed at a hotel and were scheduled to meet at the doctor's clinic. When we made it to his office, he greeted us in the waiting room. There he talked with us and told us how much he depended on God; this was when we found out he was a believer. Shortly after being introduced to him, he took us into the back room to meet his staff that was seated around in a circle; they all began to minister to us. One of them said, "You might ask why this happened to you? But it was the enemy that did this." After they ministered to us they put Puffs in the center of the group, anointed her, gave us a bottle of oil, and began to pray for her. The doctor said that they treat all of their patients this way.

"Is any sick among you? let him call for the elder of the church; and let them pray over him, anointing him with oil in the name of the Lord: And the prayer of faith shall save the sick, and the Lord shall raise him up..."
James 5:14-15

I stayed with them for the first week but I had to return home. God made a way for Denie to be able to spend the remainder of the weeks with a couple who lived there locally and had offered their home for her and Puffs to stay in with them while she underwent treatments.

Puffs' treatments in Texas lasted six weeks. Denie told me that one day while she was waiting to take Puffs in for her treatment she met an elderly woman that was accompanying her husband in the facility. They had begun talking and suddenly the woman, who was a perfect stranger, decided to give her $100. I thought to myself how awesome God is! Denie was able to make it to each of Puffs' treatments and to church every Sunday the whole time she was in Texas.

Chapter XII

The Final Test

When Denie and Puffs arrived home, Denie made an appointment to follow up with her regular doctor at Sloan Kettering. Puffs was examined again and given a blood test because she was returning to school. Once the results had returned the nurse called me at my house. I realized she must have called me because she could not reach Denie, and my number just happened to be second on the list to call regarding Puffs' condition. Unfortunately though I was not home so she left a message that said, "**THERE IS NO EVIDENCE OF THE DISEASE. Puffs can return to school.**" I will never forget that statement. This was the best news: **Puffs is a "Miracle Child."**

After the nurse left that message, a follow-up letter was sent to Denie in the mail confirming in writing the same information. So this was documented on the hospital's records, a profound miracle. Praise God!

In writing this journal to a miracle, I asked my daughter to add one key thought to encourage mothers who might be facing a 15% chance of their child living. Denie made the following statement: "I encourage mothers to trust God in your darkest moment. God is infinite in wisdom and he knows the end from the beginning. Find a spiritual song and encourage yourself in songs and hymns. I learned to worship

God in the midst of the storm and stood firm on his word. God is a miracle working God."

On June 5, 2010 Puffs celebrated her 16th birthday and had already begun making plans for her "Sweet 16 Birthday Party." She has been working very hard in high school and has taken classes, even on Saturdays, to prepare for college. God has blessed her to be a saved healthy pretty teenage girl with lots of friends. "**Miracle**" is her name: a living witness to the healing power of God.

Through this journey I experienced the peace of God and the keeping power of the Holy Spirit. I learned a valuable lesson that God's word never fails and He wants us to love and trust him. Now unto God be all the glory!!!

"For as the rain cometh down, and snow from heaven, and returneth not thither, but watereth the earth and maketh it bring forth and bud, that it may give seed to the sower, and bread to the eater: So shall my word be that goeth forth out of my mouth: it shall not return unto me void, but it shall accomplish that which I please, and it shall prosper in the thing whereto I sent it."

Isaiah 55:10-11

Made in the USA
Middletown, DE
18 April 2015